Go Wild

BE A SURVIVOR

Thanks to the creative team:
Senior Editor: Alice Peebles
Designer: Lauren Woods and collaborate agency

Hungry Tomato™
A division of Lerner Publishing Group, Inc.
241 First Avenue North
Minneapolis, MN 55401 USA

For reading levels and more information, look up this title
at www.lernerbooks.com.

Main body text set in Zemke Hand ITC 14/1.7
Typeface provided by International Typeface Corporation

Library of Congress Cataloging-in-Publication Data

Oxlade, Chris.
    Be a survivor / by Chris Oxlade ; illustrated by Eva Sassin.
        pages cm. — (Go wild)
    ISBN 978-1-4677-6356-1 (lib : alk. paper)
    ISBN 978-1-4677-7649-3 (pb : alk. paper)
    ISBN 978-1-4677-7224-2 (eb pdf)
    1. Survival—Juvenile literature. I. Title.
    GF86.O95 2016
    613.6'9—dc23   2015001939

Manufactured in the United States of America
1 – VP – 7/15/15

Go Wild

BE A SURVIVOR

By Chris Oxlade

Illustrated by Eva Sassin

HUNGRY TOMATO™

Minneapolis

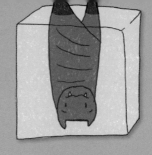

CONTENTS

TIME TO GO WILD

What do you do in an emergency? Do you know how to stay safe, take care of injuries, keep from getting lost, and find food and shelter if you're stuck outdoors? No? Then it's time to go wild! Go exploring, see amazing natural sights, have lots of fun, and learn how to survive outside! Even if you live in the middle of a city, you can have a wild time in your backyard, your local park, or another place where you have an adult's permission to explore and where it's safe and legal.

Discover some of the skills you'll need to survive in the wild: building camps, lighting fires, finding water, and signaling for help.

WILD SAFETY

- Never go exploring in the wild without an adult.

- Ask an adult before you do any of the projects in this book. In particular, ask permission before going near or in water, exploring in bad weather or in the dark, and using a GPS.

CARING FOR THE ENVIRONMENT

Always take care of the environment when you are in the wild. That means:

- Never damage rocks, animals, or plants.

- Take special care to keep fires under control and make sure a fire is out before you leave it.

SURVIVAL STUFF

THE KIT YOU NEED TO SURVIVE

You never know exactly what nature is going to throw at you when you head out into the wild! So it's wise to have a survival kit in your backpack. You can use your kit for some of the projects later in the book.

Put together a survival kit

Here are all the bits and pieces you will need.

a simple first-aid kit containing a few Band-Aids, a bandage roll, and some safety pins

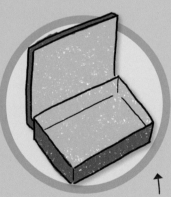

a small metal tin or a plastic box to store your survival supplies

a small mirror

a whistle

a few feet of paracord (a strong, artificial cord)

a penknife or multi-tool (ask an adult before you use this)

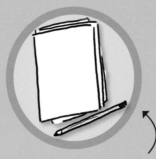

a pencil and a few small sheets of paper

flint and steel for lighting a fire

an emergency thermal blanket to keep you warm if you need to wait for help

some waterproof matches

some emergency food, such as snack bars

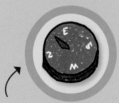

a button compass

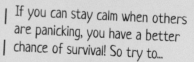

a flashlight

a few feet of fishing line and some small fishing hooks

FIGHTING FEAR

If you can stay calm when others are panicking, you have a better chance of survival! So try to...

• solve one problem at a time, starting with what's most urgent

• make practical decisions that put safety first (for example, never cross a raging river)

• prepare for the worst but hope for the best!

• never give up!

TAKE COVER!

Spider tent

BUILDING A SHELTER

The weather can be a terrible foe in the wild. Wind and rain make you cold and damp, and strong sunshine can fry you to a crisp. Luckily, it's not too tricky to craft a shelter that'll keep the elements (oh, and some wild beasts) at bay.

Argh! Bear!

A lean-to shelter

The simplest of all . . .

1. Find a tree with a branch sticking out about 3 feet (1 meter) above the ground.

2. Find a branch about 8 feet (2.5 m) long. Rest one end in the V between the tree trunk and the branch to make a top beam for your shelter.

WHERE TO BUILD?

Steer clear of windy hilltops, where you could be blown away. Also avoid areas right next to streams or in hollows, where you could be flooded out. When you're building a practice shelter near home, get an adult's OK first.

3. Lean plenty of branches at an angle from the ground against the beam on both sides.

4. Smother the branches in dead leaves or more leafy branches.

5. Throw more dry leaves on the ground to make your shelter more comfortable.

6. Snuggle inside, feet first.

An A-frame

Can't find a tree to support your shelter? Use this handy frame instead. Or use two A-frames to support a tent-shaped shelter.

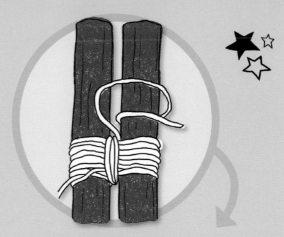

1. Tie the end of a piece of paracord to a 5-foot-long (1-meter-long) stick, about 10 inches (25 centimeters) from one end. Use a clove hitch, as shown above.

2. Put another stick next to the first one.

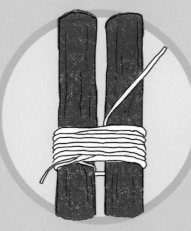

3. Wrap the cord around both sticks about 10 times, but not too tightly.

4. Wrap the cord twice around the turns of rope between the two sticks.

5. Tie the end of the rope around the second stick, again with a clove hitch.

6. That's it! Pull the ends of the sticks apart to form your A-frame.

Always ask permission before tying up a friend!

ICY IGLOOS

BUILDING SNOW SHELTERS

When it snows in the wild, you can build a simple windbreak or even an igloo using the snow itself. (Igloos are temporary shelters originally built by Inuit peoples of the Arctic.) It might be hard work that takes you a few hours, but it'll be worth the effort.

Build a snow windbreak

1. Make a snow block by packing snow into a plastic box and stamping it down firmly.

2. Put some blocks end to end to make a low, curved wall, with the outside of the wall facing the wind.

3. Add a second layer of blocks to make the wall higher. Keep adding layers until the wall is high enough to crouch behind. Stuff snow into any gaps.

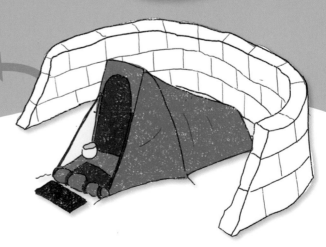

Make an igloo shelter

IGLOO SAFETY
Don't make the igloo too big. Ice blocks can be heavy, and you don't want them to trap you if the igloo collapses!

1. Mark a circle in the snow about 3 feet (1 m) across.

2. Make snow blocks (see Step 1, left page) and build a snow wall around the circle, leaving a gap for a door. You could start with the snow wall you built before.

3. Add more blocks to make another layer of your wall, but place these blocks at a slight angle so the wall leans in a little.

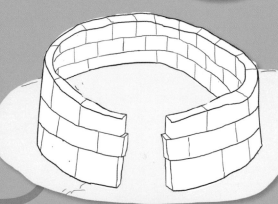

4. Once you've arranged four or five layers of blocks, you'll need an assistant to support the blocks as you put them in place.

5. Add a capping block to fill the hole in the roof of your igloo. Next, stuff snow into any gaps.

6. You can improve your igloo by adding a tunnel at the entrance.

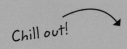

Chill out!

WILD WARMTH

MAKING A FIRE

Fire is a lifesaver in the wild. It keeps you warm in cold weather, cooks food, lights up the dark, and wards off wild animals. To start a fire you need fuel, heat, and air.

FIRE SAFETY

Always ask an adult before lighting a fire, whether you're in a backyard or in the wild. Don't light fires when the weather has been very dry, and don't make your fire so large that it could get out of control.

Don't let your tail catch fire!

Lighting a fire

1. Choose a site for your fire that's well away from trees. Clear the ground and cut away turf so you can put it back later.

2. Gather tinder, kindling, and fuel (see page 13).

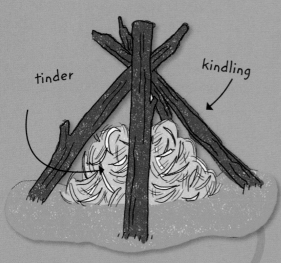

tinder

kindling

4. Light the tinder with a match. As the tinder begins to burn, add more tinder. Then add kindling.

5. Look after your fire, feeding it with kindling regularly.

6. Always make sure your fire is out and the ashes are cold before you leave. Clear the site and replace turf if you have cut it.

3. Lay a mat of dry, dead wood, then arrange your kindling into a small tepee, with the tinder underneath.

Make a feather stick

Make a feather stick if you can't find any small kindling to get your fire going.

1. Find a dry stick about half an inch (1 cm) thick. Use your knife to cut slivers of wood along the sides, so the stick looks feathery.

2. Make a few feather sticks and keep them ready in case you want to light a fire in a hurry.

BE SAFE

Read page 16 for knife safety tips before you start.

tinder

FIRE FUEL

To get a fire going, you need:

Tinder: fluffy material that burns very easily, such as dry grass

Kindling: small twigs and other pieces of wood

Fuel: sticks and logs

It's nice to share your fire with friends.

Fire without matches

You won't find one of these in the wild!

What happens if you drop your matches in a pond? Don't despair. You can still light a fire without them!

1. A flint and steel is made up of a strip of magnesium metal and a steel striker.

2. To light tinder with a flint and steel, aim the flint at the tinder, press the steel onto the flint, and push the steel down to make a spark. Keep trying until the tinder lights.

3. Once your tinder is smoldering, blow gently to make it burst into flames. Now you can put kindling over the tinder and get your fire going.

4. On a hot, sunny day, you can also light a fire with a magnifying glass. Focus the sun's rays onto tinder until it smolders, then blow on the tinder as before.

Fire by friction

This fire-lighting method was invented thousands of years ago. It's tricky, but give it a try!

socket

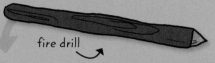
fire drill

1. Make a fire drill from a straight stick about 20 inches (50 cm) long. Sharpen one end and make the other end rounded.

bow

2. Make a bow from a curved branch and some paracord or strong string. The string should be taut but not too tight.

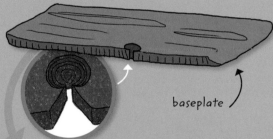
baseplate

3. Cut a triangular notch about an inch (2.5 cm) deep into the side of a wooden baseplate.

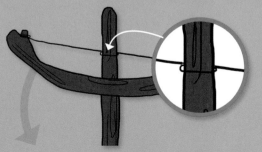

4. Wrap the string of your bow once around your drill. Place the sharp end of the drill into the notch on the baseplate.

5. Press down on top of the stick with a concave stone (one with a small hollow).

6. Ready to make fire? Move the bow backward and forward quickly. After a while, you should get black powder in the notch and a scorched hole in the wood.

7. Gradually move the bow faster and faster until the drill begins to smoke. Go faster still, and you should produce a glowing ember in the pile of powder.

8. Transfer the ember to a heap of kindling and blow gently to make flames.

CHOP IT UP

USING A KNIFE

In the wild, you often need to make stuff from the bits of wood you find around you. So you need a knife and the skills to use it properly.

penknife

sheath knife

Using a penknife safely

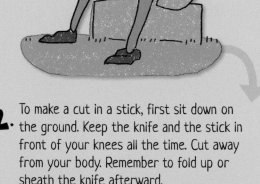

1. Here's how to hold a knife safely. This forehand grip allows you to push down firmly on the knife and make a cut.

2. To make a cut in a stick, first sit down on the ground. Keep the knife and the stick in front of your knees all the time. Cut away from your body. Remember to fold up or sheath the knife afterward.

3. To make deeper cuts or cut harder wood, rest the stick on a tree trunk or large log. The other rules still apply — always cut away from your body.

Making a walking stick

So heavy!

1. Find a branch about an inch (2.5 cm) thick and about 5 feet (1.5 m) long. Ask an adult to saw off the ends if you can only find a longer branch.

3. Make similar cuts at the other end of the branch, but this time, form a blunt end.

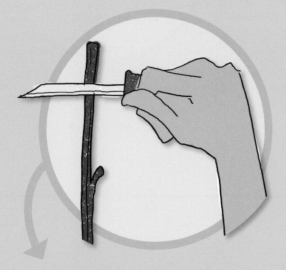

2. Cut diagonally through the branch near one end. Make more cuts to form a sharp point. Make several small cuts rather than one or two big ones.

4. Decorate your stick by cutting notches along the sides. To make a notch, rest your stick on a tree trunk or log, make a shallow cut at an angle. Next, angle the blade the other way and make another cut. Remove the waste wood.

Walking sticks aren't very helpful when you're a bird!

Left! Left! Left, right, left!

THIRSTY WORK

FINDING WATER

You can't survive without water. So if you're in the wild, gasping for a drink—but there isn't a clean river or stream close by—tyou need to know how to find water.

WATER SAFETY

Never drink water you've found in the wild without sterilizing it first (with special tablets or by boiling it). Never drink salt water. And never drink your own pee.

Water from leaves

Water is always evaporating from the leaves of plants. And you can capture it.

Remember to remove bugs before you sterilize your water!

1. Carefully put a clear plastic bag over the end of a branch of a tree or shrub. Close the neck of the bag and tie it loosely with string.

2. Wait for a few hours, then examine the bag. You should find that water has collected in the bottom.

Water from grass

Collect dew from the grass in the early morning by tying towels to your legs and walking around. Then simply squeeze the water from the towel.

Water from the Sun

Get water using the sun's energy!

1. Find a sunny spot and dig a shallow pit, about a foot (30 cm) deep in the ground. Place a dish or another container in the center of the pit.

2. Cover the pit with a plastic sheet. Put stones around the edge to hold the plastic sheet in place. Place a small stone in the center of the sheet to make it sag slightly in the middle. Put some fresh leaves in the pit too.

3. Wait a few hours. Then look in the container. Do you have any water?

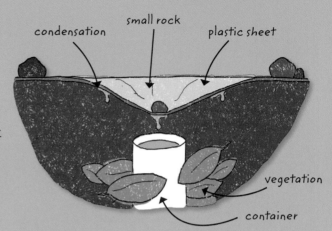

condensation   small rock   plastic sheet

vegetation

container

Water from a frog

In a dire emergency, you can get water from a frog's body. Only try this under expert supervision, and only in a real emergency!

1. First you have to find the right sort of frog, such as the water-holding frog that lives in Australia! This normally means digging into the ground.

2. Squeeze the frog gently sideways and be ready to catch the water in a dish or in your mouth!

Collecting rainwater

Tie the corners of a plastic sheet to the branches of a tree, with one end of the sheet lower than the other. If it rains, water will pour off the sheet. Catch it in a container.

CATCHING A FEAST

HUNTING AND FISHING

So you've built a shelter, found some water, and gotten your fire going. All you need now is something to eat! Don't catch any animals to eat unless it's a real survival situation.

Don't eat us!
We are poisonous!

Make a bottle fish trap

2. Reverse the top and push it into the bottle.

3. Put some bait, such as food scraps, into the bottle.

4. Place your trap underwater for a few hours. Look inside. Any fish?

1. Cut the top off a plastic soda pop bottle.

Make a slingshot

Here's a hunting tool you could use in a survival situation. Never fire this at any animal (or person) if you're not actually starving in the wilderness.

1. Find a tree branch with a neat Y shape, like this one. The wood should be at least half an inch (1 cm) thick.

2. With a knife or saw, cut away the ends to make a Y-shaped piece of wood about 8 inches (20 cm) long.

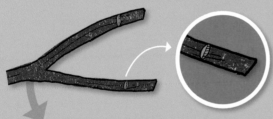

3. Cut a shallow notch about an inch (2.5 cm) from the end of each arm.

4. Prepare a piece of nylon webbing, or a leather strip, about 5 inches (12 cm) long. Cut a hole about an inch (2.5 cm) from each end.

5. Now you need a length of thick elastic or rubber tubing, about 2 feet (60 cm) long. Thread the elastic through the holes in the webbing.

6. Tie the ends of the elastic around the top of the arms of the Y shape in line with notches.

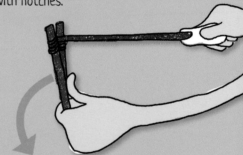

7. To fire your slingshot, put a small stone in the center of the webbing, grip the stone through the webbing from behind, pull back the webbing, take aim . . . and fire!

This might be a bit more that he bargained for!

Make a fishing rod

flying fish

1. Look for a bendy stick at least 6 feet (2 m) long. Cut a small notch close to the thinner end.

2. Tie a length of string about 6 feet (2 m) long to the thin end of the stick where you cut the notch.

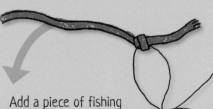

3. Add a piece of fishing line about 6 feet (2 m) long to the end of the string. To join the string and line, double over the end of the line and tie a loop, then tie the string to the loop.

4. Now tie a fishing hook to the line with a half blood knot, as shown.

1

2

3

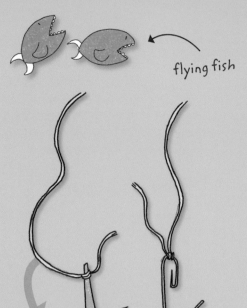

5. If you don't have a fishing hook or a line, don't despair! You can make hooks from paper clips and even the thorns from prickly plants such as hawthorn.

6. You can also try fishing with any sort of cord, such as string, cotton, wool, and even your shoe laces.

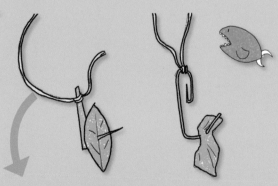

7. For bait you can use food scraps or objects that look like a small fish underwater.

8. Drop your hook and bait into the water. Now wait patiently. If your line wiggles, pull up sharply on the fishing rod to hook the fish.

IF YOU CATCH A FISH...

Wet your hands and hold the fish firmly but not tightly. Carefully remove the hook from the fish's mouth, then return the fish to the water if you're not going to eat it. Always release fish that you don't need for survival.

Spit fishing

1. Stand in the water and spit into the area in front of you.

2. Wait with your T-shirt ready to scoop up fish attracted to the spit. Simple!

FISHING, SAFETY, AND THE LAW

Never go fishing without an adult, and never fish where there is a chance of falling into deep, cold, or fast-flowing water. Also be careful of sharp hooks. You should use barbless hooks, which are easier to get out of fish and fingers than barbed ones. Make sure you know the local laws about fishing. In many places you need a license to fish.

Fishing by hand

1. Stand very still in shallow water, up to a foot (30 cm) deep, with your hands cupped.

2. Wait for a fish to come close. Then very, very slowly, move your hands around it, and grab it!

23

WILD FARE

FORAGING FOR FOOD

Plants are on the menu in the wild. So are fish and other animals. And catching plants is much easier than catching animals! Check out some of the yummy berries, nuts, and leaves you can eat.

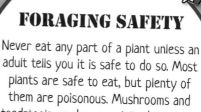
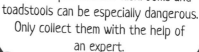

FORAGING SAFETY

Never eat any part of a plant unless an adult tells you it is safe to do so. Most plants are safe to eat, but plenty of them are poisonous. Mushrooms and toadstools can be especially dangerous. Only collect them with the help of an expert.

Collecting berries and nuts

Nuts and berries are a good source of energy.

1. Blackberries, blueberries, and cranberries are all edible. You can eat them raw or stew them in a pot over your campfire.

2. Search for nuts, such as hazelnuts and sweet chestnuts, which you can eat raw. Collect acorns too, but boil them a few times in water so they won't taste bitter.

blueberries

blackberries

cranberries

hazelnuts

acorns

sweet chestnuts

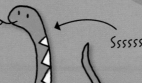

Ssssssssso tasty!

Collecting leaves

Eating leaves might not seem like a good idea, but many herbs are leaves, and so are many salad ingredients. You can find similar leaves to eat in the wild.

1. Search for dandelion, sorrel, and stinging nettle leaves. You can also eat watercress if you find it near rivers.

dandelion

sorrel (usually has three leaves in the wild)

stinging nettle

2. You can make delicious tea from stinging nettles. Pick the leaves of young plants, wearing gloves to avoid being stung. Wash the leaves with fresh water.

3. Put the leaves in a pan of boiling water and boil them for a few minutes, until the water looks slightly green. Allow the water to cool a little before drinking. Don't worry—the nettles can't sting any more!

I shouldn't have eaten ALL the blackberries!

Don't eat me! I am purple, but I am not a blackberry!

FOOD ON FIRE

COOKING OVER A CAMPFIRE

If you've found some food to eat in the wild, you can make a fire (see page 12) and cook the food over it. To practice cooking over a fire, try these projects with food from home.

Make a pot support

Want to heat and purify water in a pot? Here's how to suspend a kettle over a fire.

1. Find a stick or branch with a fork in it. Shorten the ends to make a stick with a forked end, about 20 inches (50 cm) long. Sharpen the single end.

2. Push the stick into the ground close to your fire, but not so close that it will burn.

3. Find a stick about 5 feet (1.5 m) long. Cut off the side branches, then cut a deep notch about an inch (2.5 cm) from the thin end of the stick.

4. Place the long stick in the support. One end should rest on the ground. The other end should be over the fire, high enough up so that it doesn't burn. Use a log or a large stone to hold the stick steady.

Now you can make some nettle tea (see page 25)!

5. Hang your kettle in the notch, being careful of the fire.

Cooking in foil

Use this method for cooking potatoes and other vegetables in your fire.

1. Wrap your baking or sweet potatoes in foil and drop them in the middle of the fire. Keep your hands away from the flames.

2. Give the vegetables half an hour to cook. Use a stick to roll them out of the fire, then ask an adult to unwrap them.

Making a skewer

Any food that you can put on a skewer can be cooked over your fire. That includes marshmallows, sausages, and vegetables.

1. Make a support, as in Step 1 on the left page.

2. Find thin, green sticks and shave off the bark to make skewers.

Even when cooked, worms will probably be icky!

3. Attach a skewer to a longer stick by wrapping string around both. Push your food onto the skewer and rest the stick in the support so that the food is over the fire.

I'm a survival chef!

SOS!

Don't light your fire until you are ready!

CALLING FOR HELP

If you're trapped or lost in the wild, you need to know how to call for help. Remember that there probably won't be a phone signal where you are. Or you might have dropped your phone into a river! Never call for help unless there is a real emergency.

Fire signals

Bright flames will attract rescuers at night, and smoke will attract rescuers in daytime. Light your rescue fire in a clearing on a hilltop.

1. First, gather up all the fuel you need for a fire. Next, build a fuel pile that is ready to light (see page 12).

2. Keep a lookout. Only light your fire when help is in sight. During the day, make smoke by putting branches with green leaves over the fire.

3. Remember to put the fire out after you've been rescued.

Make a heliograph

You can use a mirror, which you should have in your survival kit, to send signals using light from the sun. (You can also use a metal tin or a pair of glasses.) This is called a heliograph.

1. Hold the heliograph so that it bounces sunlight toward the ground. Practice moving the spot by tilting the heliograph left and right or up and down.

2. To signal an aircraft, send an SOS with three short flashes, three long flashes, and three short flashes again.

Ground signals

Place signals on the ground by arranging logs or branches to make shapes that can be seen from the air.

1. Find a large open space that can be seen from the air.

2. Make a signal as large as possible using branches, by clearing leaves, or by tramping hollows in snow.

serious injury

need food and water

yes

no

unable to move

moving this way

all is well

DID YOU KNOW?

○ Humans discovered how to light fires at least one million years ago. Traces of these fires have been found in a cave in South Africa.

○ You can make fire from ice! Simply find a slab of very clear ice, shape it into a convex lens, and use it to focus sunlight onto tinder.

○ You can also make fire using an empty drink can. Use the dish-shaped base to focus sunlight onto tinder.

○ Have you heard of the fire triangle? It's includes the three things you need to get a fire going: fuel, oxygen (from the air), and heat.

○ Around 15,000 years ago, humans who lived by hunting and gathering made dome-shaped shelters from the huge bones of mammoths.

○ The largest igloo ever built was made by an adventure sports company in Canada in 2011. It measured more than 30 feet (9 m) across and contained 2,500 blocks of snow.

○ In 2003, Aron Ralston was exploring a canyon in Utah when a massive boulder fell and pinned his arm. After a few days, he realized the only way to survive was to cut off his arm with his outdoor knife. The movie *127 Hours* is based on his frightening experience.

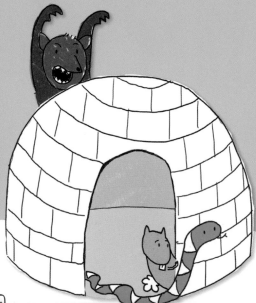

British mountaineer Joe Simpson was climbing in the Andes when he fell and broke his leg. He later slipped into a crevasse. He was in terrible pain, with no food or water, but he crawled back to safety. It took him four days.

Scotsman Alexander Selkirk was left alone on a Pacific island in 1704. He survived there for four and a half years before being rescued. The famous book *Robinson Crusoe* is based on Selkirk's adventure.

You need to drink 4 pints (2 liters) of water a day to stay healthy. That's about eight glasses full. You should drink more when the weather's hot or when you're doing strenuous exercise.

People have survived without water by drinking their own pee. But it's a last resort and is only safe for a day or two. Don't try it!

The slingshot, or catapult, became a popular toy after inflatable tires were invented in 1888. Children used old inner tubes for slingshot elastic.

The rosary pea, native to India, is the most poisonous plant that exists. The plant's red and black seeds contain a deadly chemical.

In 1894, soldiers of the US Army sent a message between two hilltops 183 miles (295 km) apart using mirrors to reflect the sun.

Oh no!
Not again!

INDEX

THE AUTHOR

Chris Oxlade is an experienced author of educational books for children. He has written more than two hundred books on science, technology, sports and hobbies, including many activity and project books. He enjoys camping and adventurous outdoor sports including rock climbing, hill running, kayaking, and sailing. He lives in England with his wife, children, and dogs.

THE ARTIST

Eva Sassin is a freelance illustrator born and bred in London, England. She has loved illustrating ever since she can remember, and she loves combining characters with unusual textures to give them more depth and keep them interesting.